CHATELAINE
home decor

CLASSIC
CHIC

CLASSIC CHIC

Timeless decorating that's always in style

M&S

A SMITH SHERMAN BOOK
produced in conjunction with CHATELAINE®
and published by McCLELLAND & STEWART INC.

CHATELAINE

Canadian Cataloguing in Publication Data

Mackie, Joan
    Classic chic : timeless decorating that's always in style

(Chatelaine home decor)
"A Smith Sherman book produced in conjunction with Chatelaine"
Written by Joan Mackie—cf. Acknowledgements.
Includes index.

ISBN 0-7710-2009-0

1. Interior Decoration   I. Title.   II. Series.

NK2115.M223 1999   747   C99-931694-X

ACKNOWLEDGEMENTS

Classic Chic would not have been possible without Joan Mackie. As the former homes editor of *Chatelaine* magazine, she produced the features and wrote this book. Our thanks to her.

As well, we would like to thank the designers and homeowners who allowed us to reproduce their work and homes, and Ted Yarwood and Evan Dion for photographing them so beautifully.

We are also grateful to Rona Maynard, editor of *Chatelaine*, group publisher Lee Simpson and brand development director Cheryl Smith. Thanks to Caren Watkins, *Chatelaine's* art director, Ann Shier, associate art director, and creative associate Barbara Glaser.

Thanks to Deborah Aldcorn and Bernice Eisenstein for their keen eyes and attention to detail, Joseph Gisini for his creativity and everyone at McClelland & Stewart.

COVER PHOTO: *see page 20*

PHOTO PAGE 2: *see page 110*

CREDITS: *see page 125*

CONTENTS

continued on next page

DENS

INTRODUCTION

WHAT IS A CLASSIC? The dictionary will tell you it's anything that is timeless and that serves as a standard of excellence. Architectural books will talk about Greece and Rome. Simply put, a classic is anything that has endured time and changing fashions to remain just that — a classic. It's not dated-looking or trendy. A classic is characterized by design principles that govern scale, size, shape, materials and color. Just mention a Chanel suit, Katharine Hepburn or a Duncan Phyfe table and people know what you're talking about when you talk about a classic.

In *Classic Chic*, we take elements of classic styles and throw in lots of panache to help you decorate rooms that won't suffer from the "museum look." It is obvious that decorating with select classics is the chic thing to do today, and the most successful scheme results when you combine classic pieces with objects from several periods in the past and with objects made today, rather than drawing solely on one period. In this way,

you will produce spaces that appear to have evolved gradually over time.

Classic Chic shows you how to use existing furnishings to give your home the classic look. Look around the house; check in the basement and attic. You may find some classic pieces waiting to be mixed in with your current furnishings. Don't worry if they need a little touching up — we even tell you how to do that.

Classics fall into a number of styles and sub-styles, but mainly they can be viewed — as a result of shared characteristics — as being traditional (or formal) or country in persuasion. This book reflects these groupings and the various details that put a classic into its category are evident in the glorious pictures that fill the following pages.

So turn the pages, revel in the scenes revealed throughout this book and enjoy the rooms that classics have created. Or get out your tools and create some classic touches for your home.

Entrances
OPENING REMARKS

*A*NY ENTRANCE THAT'S decorated in a classic style sets the tone for the entire house. Because of the timeless qualities of classics, the most immediate feeling one will experience is that of being in a very comfortable place. Things just "feel" right.

When you decorate with pieces whose history stretches way back, as the history behind classics does, your successfully decorated room will be more assured. The lines and colors of classics were admired for their beauty when they were first made. They will be equally appealing today as they were when they first came into favor.

The traditionally furnished entrance opposite is a case in point. The downsized reproduction bow-fronted table (perfectly scaled for today's smaller entrances), federal-style mirror and brass accessories add up to a classic composition, which looks reassuringly familiar and therefore welcoming, even though you may never before have seen a room decorated exactly this way.

Equally friendly, though totally different, the country-look entrance on page 13 warmly greets visitors in its own classic way. The honey tones of the wood and the casual, colorful wildflower

TINY TRADITIONAL ENTRANCE
A petite but pretty entrance gives a big welcome when its accent pieces are filled with flair. Oversized tousled topiaries fashioned from dried flowers accessorize a small bow-fronted reproduction antique table; a small-scale gilded federal-style mirror crowns the formal arrangement.

bouquet brighten up an otherwise dark area. With a country look, nothing feels intimidating, so the welcome is guaranteed to be open and friendly.

Not every item in an entrance must be a "classic" for the space to be considered successful. One or two larger pieces (a table, chair or mirror, for instance) or smaller accessories may be all that is necessary to create the ambience and establish a place that's inviting. ✤

SUNSHINE-WARM WELCOME
Butter-yellow walls warm up the welcome quotient of a classic country-look entrance and show off a honey-hued pine washstand and mirror. A cheery bouquet of pastel-colored flowers overflows an earthenware jug. The pine-framed mirror, adapted from an old cupboard door, reflects botanical prints hanging on the opposite wall.

HOMESTEADER WELCOME

Furnishings saved from the homes of early settlers create a warm welcome in a classic way. In the early 20th century, a Doukhobor prayer table, similar to the one here, would have held the elements of life — water, bread and salt — during religious meetings. Today, just inside a country-home entrance door, it's topped with a folk-art horse and wagon, a painted box and a Ukrainian lamp shelf. Underneath, a stack of Hutterite baskets and a handwoven rug add to the country welcome.

STRIPE IT RICH

Stripes on walls and faux-marble painted on a shelf — two classic decorating devices — combine to produce an expensive look in a small but chic entranceway. The gilded mirror and the rich grains in the wooden boxes decorating the shelf enhance the drama introduced by the emerald-green paint. Every entrance benefits from having a place to set down gloves, keys and letters; one as elegant as this becomes a work of art in its own right.

PROJECTS

SHELVE IT — COUNTRY STYLE

Use demolition discards to create a shelf.

1. Wearing disposable gloves, remove old paint or varnish from discarded brackets using paint stripper, a scraper and medium-grade steel wool according to the manufacturer's instructions on the product. Sand smooth and remove dust with the tack cloth.

2. Sand the shelf until smooth. Remove dust with the tack cloth. Glue the brackets to the shelf and let dry, then attach two screws through each bracket into the underside of the shelf.

3. Apply two or three coats of paint or varnish. Let dry and sand between coats or apply furniture polish according to the manufacturer's instructions.

4. Sand the 1 x 1-inch length of wood and finish the same way as the shelf. Use three screws to attach it to the wall, centring it where you want the centre of the shelf to be. Rest the shelf on top of it, then attach the shelf to the wood with three screws.

SHOPPING LIST

- *discarded wooden brackets, available at demolition yards*
- *disposable latex gloves*
- *paint stripper*
- *scraper*
- *medium-grade steel wool*
- *medium- and fine-grit sandpaper*
- *tack cloth*
- *1½-inch (3.8-cm) thick piece of wood for shelf, cut to desired depth and length*
- *carpenters' glue*
- *two 1½-inch (3.8-cm) screws*
- *screwdriver*
- *varnish, latex paint or furniture wax to finish*
- *1-inch (2.5-cm) paintbrush if using varnish or paint*
- *piece of wood 1 x 1 inch and half the length of the shelf*
- *six 2-inch (5-cm) screws*

MAKE AN ENTRANCE
Traditional details decorate a
plain wooden door.

SHOPPING LIST
- *wood moldings of different depths,*
  widths and profiles
- *wood baseboard molding*
- *mitre box*
- *backsaw*
- *fine-grit sandpaper*
- *wood door*
- *carpenters' glue*
- *small finishing nails*
- *hammer*
- *awl*
- *Polyfilla*
- *tack cloth*
- *2-inch (5-cm) paintbrush*
- *small amount of latex primer paint,*
  less than 1 quart (1 L)
- *1 quart (1 L) latex semigloss paint*
  (use exterior paint for exterior door;
  for interior door, use interior paint)

---

1. Draw or sketch on paper the design you want to create on your door. Take this to the lumberyard or building-supply store and get sales help in buying the required quantities of moldings.

2. Using a mitre box set at 45 degrees, saw pieces of molding strips to fit the pattern you want to create. Sand the ends smooth.

3. Glue the pieces to the door, then hammer two or three small nails in each piece to hold them firmly in place. Let the glue dry. Use an awl and hammer to countersink the nails below the surface of the moldings. Use Polyfilla to fill in any cracks at the corner joins and where the nails were countersunk.

4. Sand the door and moldings. Remove dust with the tack cloth.

5. Apply one coat of primer. Let dry, sand the door, wipe with the tack cloth, then apply two or three coats of paint. Let dry, sand and wipe between coats.

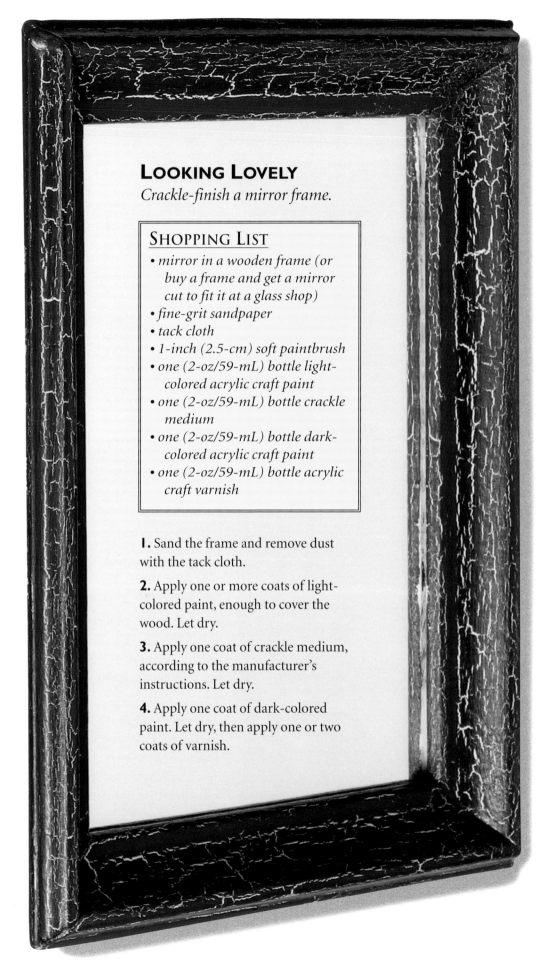

LOOKING LOVELY

Crackle-finish a mirror frame.

SHOPPING LIST

- *mirror in a wooden frame (or buy a frame and get a mirror cut to fit it at a glass shop)*
- *fine-grit sandpaper*
- *tack cloth*
- *1-inch (2.5-cm) soft paintbrush*
- *one (2-oz/59-mL) bottle light-colored acrylic craft paint*
- *one (2-oz/59-mL) bottle crackle medium*
- *one (2-oz/59-mL) bottle dark-colored acrylic craft paint*
- *one (2-oz/59-mL) bottle acrylic craft varnish*

1. Sand the frame and remove dust with the tack cloth.

2. Apply one or more coats of light-colored paint, enough to cover the wood. Let dry.

3. Apply one coat of crackle medium, according to the manufacturer's instructions. Let dry.

4. Apply one coat of dark-colored paint. Let dry, then apply one or two coats of varnish.

WELCOME MAT

Braid a rug for a country welcome.

SHOPPING LIST

- cotton fabric in assorted
  colors and patterns
  *(Note: 12 yards (11 metres)
  of 45-inch-wide (115-cm)
  fabric will make a
  24-yard-long (22-metre)
  braid, which coils into a
  rug measuring 36 x 24
  inches (1 m x 60 cm)*
- scissors
- thread
- extra-strong thread and
  heavy needle

1. Cut bias strips of fabric, 4 inches (10 cm) wide. To cut fabric on the bias, lay a large piece on a flat surface. Taking a corner edge, fold it so the entire length of the bottom edge lies flat and even along a long side edge. Press this diagonal fold in place with your hands so there's a line along which to make your first scissor cut. Cut the fabric at this line, then measure 4 inches (10 cm) and make a cut parallel to the first. Continue cutting in this way. This will give you strips 4 inches (10 cm) wide.

2. Sew the short ends of the fabric together in ¼-inch (0.5-cm) seams, right-sides together, to create very long strips. Take three strips and pin their ends together. This will be the start of the braid.

3. Begin braiding, turning under the raw edges of the fabric as you braid. Sew on more strips as required.

4. When you think you have enough fabric braided to complete the rug, use extra-strong thread and a sturdy needle to hand-sew the braid together on the underside. Depending on how you coil the braid, you can create a round or oval rug. You can continue adding to the braid after you have started sewing it together if you decide to increase its size. Tuck the final ends of the braid to the underside and sew firmly in place.

Living Rooms
LUXURY SPACE

*T*HERE'S A FEELING of indefinable luxury in living rooms decorated with classics. Perhaps it's the sense of timelessness that classics intrinsically impart that creates this feeling. Whether the room is "traditional" or "country" in flavor, the comfort level is high and anyone relaxing in one of these rooms feels this all-pervasive comfort.

In the living room opposite, paisley and faded chintz — two enduring classic motifs — and a kilim carpet and stool combine for an elegant, traditional room. In another traditionally decorated room on pages 22 and 23, only the round table between the two armchairs is a true antique. The remaining furnishings are reproductions of classics, some down-scaled to fit this rather small room. The gilded mirror and red draperies contribute to the classic ambience.

The living room on page 25 shows the vibrant impact of incorporating classics from several periods and styles and updating them with contemporary fabrics. A beautiful wood-framed Victorian sofa pops to life with a spunky over-scaled strawberry print fabric. The same fabric covers a modern classic — a Lawson-style sofa.

Country classics take many forms, as several living rooms here prove. Humble wicker — an eternal favorite — decorates one room in a simple, casual way on page 37. It's the accessories with country flavor that create a classic mood in the living room on page 24. And in the living room on pages 32 and 33, settler furnishings, handmade at the turn of the century, show how immigrants from Eastern European countries, using rudimentary tools and materials, sought to recreate the classics they had left behind. ✧

ENGLISH ELEGANCE
Muted colors in floral fabrics mingle with subtle plaids and paisleys in a gracious and traditional English-inspired living room. The classic lines of the furniture and the historic subjects of the paintings stand out against soft green walls. Flowers and antique accessories from several periods add layers to the traditional look.

TIMELESS TREATMENT

A classic window treatment in Chinese-red-patterned fabric injects energy into a traditional room. Formal pleated valances top the ceiling-height side panels, which draw together for privacy or coziness. A bow-fronted chest topped by a gilded mirror and an antique table serving two traditional armchairs hold antiques and other accent pieces, some old, some new. The subtle tone-on-tone classic pattern woven in the wall-to-wall carpet expands the perceived size of the space. Decorated with a limited color palette, the room imparts a sense of timeless elegance.

CONTEMPORARY COUNTRY CHARM

Colored glass set in a pine window frame, reclaimed from a
demolished church, establishes the palette in a flower-fresh,
light-filled country-house living room. A brass pitcher makes
a fitting lamp when electrified and topped by a blue ribbon-
banded shade. Dried hydrangea flowers tumble with relaxed
abandon from their vase. Few genuine antiques dot the room,
but the overall ambience is one of simplified country.

DYNAMIC DRAMA

Touches of whimsy and elements of formality contained
within dramatic dark red walls create a stunning, timeless
living room. Over-sized strawberry plants decorate the
fabric covering traditional Lawson-style sofas and a
formal Victorian settee. A pastoral oil painting with a
contemporary flavor dominates one wall. Balancing these
strong images, a leaf-patterned carpet covers the floor, its
dark color the perfect foil for the exuberance around it.

HOT CLASSIC COUNTRY
Spicy red walls paired with raffia-colored wainscotting make a warm background for country furnishings. A chic, stylized Roman shade and sheer café curtains dress the window simply. Pine furniture, a sink-into sofa and casual accessories anchored by a rough sisal carpet create an inviting, relaxing room that brims with country flavor.

ELEGANTLY FEMININE

A Victorian sofa upholstered in white anchors a traditional room where subtle accents combine to create a calm retreat. Silk cushions and a wool carpet — all in shades of white — contrast with the dark floor and mahogany on the sofa. Gilded frames with classic details add sparkle; pearl swags embellishing the window coverings are playfully chic.

ARTS-AND-CRAFTS CLASSIC

Arts-and-crafts-style wallpaper tops paneling from the same period in a pretty pastel living room. Pink and blue flowers in myriad guises decorate the furniture, cushions, carpet, wall sconces and even the bouquet in the Chinese ginger jar on the coffee table. The cohesive result is a modern interpretation of a particular period and style — a distinctive classic — popular at the turn of the century.

CLASSIC DETAILS

Molding strips nailed to the walls create a paneled look for a room exuberantly decorated in a traditional fashion. Sets of framed botanical prints and an antique candle sconce enhance the defined areas. Muted-colored fabrics cover the furniture, whose classic lines are slightly exaggerated to please modern-day tastes, particularly on the scroll arms of the two-seater sofa. Every accessory adds up to elegance; some are genuine antiques, such as the turned candlesticks against the wall and the Regency commode topped with a samovar-shaped lamp on the left; some are reproduction pieces evocative of earlier styles, such as the demi-lune tables and chest-on-legs fronting the sofa.

HERITAGE CLASSICS

Highly prized furniture embellished with fine carving and vibrant colors parades its pedigrees in a country living room. Originally simple furniture made by homesteaders, it has, over the years, become greatly desired for its inherent sense of style. The red paint on the Russian Mennonite daybed has lost none of its impact since it was made in rural Manitoba in the 1890s. In front of it, a scalloped stretcher base connects the legs of a two-drawer Ukrainian kitchen table, also from Manitoba. Behind, a Doukhobor boot bench (ca. 1915) from Castlegar, B.C., has curvaceously carved edges on its ends and side pieces.

CLASSY COMFORT

Scroll-back "campaign" chairs, interpreted in modern metal, balance a traditional-styled sofa in a classy cozy living room. Nearly all the furnishings are new, but the look they create is classic. Vintage fabrics and patterned needlepoint cover the toss cushions; a Victorian screen adds depth, scale and interest behind the sofa. The wide window — an imposing but less-than-perfect feature in the room — hides behind an expanse of gathered sheers and a softly pleated valance with matching formal side panels. Carefully chosen accent pieces on the tables are all traditionally inspired.

GARDEN-STYLE LIVING

Patterns plucked from the garden set a living room
abloom. A pair of matching sofas flanks a classic fireplace;
its formal mantel and gilt-framed mirror combine to
make a major statement. Pairs of botanical prints, tole
lamps and tapestry-covered armchairs combine with a
patterned carpet and flower-decked needlepoint cushions
for a traditional look that is timeless.

COZY CORNER

Pine plank floors underscore a cozy nook whose country furnishings glow in the late-afternoon sunlight. A wicker chaise softened by plump pillows and a handwoven afghan invites one to curl up with a book and a bowl of popcorn, both within easy reach on the nearby antique-cloth-topped table. The enduring charm of wicker has given pleasure to several generations of homeowners around the world.

ELEGANT COUNTRY
French- and English-country influences inform a pretty, patterned living room, whose most formal accent is a set of framed architectural prints flanking the lace-curtained window. A muted yellow-checked fabric with French-country overtones covers a bergère chair; faded flowers and grapes decorate the fabric covering the sofa and cushions on the ladder-back chairs. An ornately carved fireplace surround adds classic elegance without overly formalizing the room.

Living Room
PROJECTS

COLORFUL COUNTRY FLOOR WARMER

A quilted rug brightens any classic country room.

1. Browse through books of traditional quilt patterns to find one that you like. Decide on the size of your rug and draw it to scale on a piece of graph paper. Use colored marker pens to define your pattern. This will indicate the number of variously shaped pieces you must cut out of several pieces of differently colored fabrics.

2. Cut out the fabric pieces, allowing an additional ¼ inch (0.5 cm) on all sides of each piece for a hem allowance.

3. Machine-sew the pieces together by placing the fabric pieces right-sides together and allowing a ¼-inch (0.5-cm) hem. Press the individual seams open before joining the seamed pieces together. Continue sewing pieces together until you have created the entire top of your quilt. Press flat.

4. Cut out a piece of cotton fabric the same size as the pieced top for backing. Repeat, using the cotton flannelette fabric for "stuffing."

5. Lay the backing piece wrong-side up on a flat surface. Lay the flannelette on top of that. Lay the pieced quilt top on top of that, right-side up.

6. Pin the three layers together, then baste with long running stitches in rows about 6 inches (15 cm) apart. Remove the pins. The basting will hold the three layers together while you are quilting.

7. "Quilt" the rug by hand-sewing with white thread through all three layers, about 6 stitches per inch (2.5 cm), or use the sewing machine. The quilting pattern can be as elaborate as you like. (Consult quilt designs in books.) Or simply follow the seam lines about ⅛ inch (3 mm) from where the pieces are joined together.

8. When the quilting is complete, cut the outer edges neatly and sew bias binding around the edges to hold the three layers together.

9. Cut a piece of anti-slip carpet underpadding 1 inch (2.5 cm) smaller than the rug and tack in place on the underside.

SHOPPING LIST
- *books of traditional quilt patterns, for inspiration*
- *graph paper*
- *colored marker pens*
- *scraps of cotton fabrics in several colors*
- *scissors*
- *large piece of cotton fabric for backing*
- *large piece of flannelette for padding*
- *white thread*
- *small fine needle*
- *bias binding*
- *anti-slip carpet underpadding*

FRINGE BENEFITS

Easy dress-ups for basic cushions.

1. Measure the perimeter of cushions to determine the amount of fringe required. Add 1 extra inch (2.5 cm) for overlapping the ends and turning corners.

2. Sew the fringe to the cushion edges using color-matched thread and small stitches. Turn under the ends and sew carefully to prevent fraying.

SHOPPING LIST
- *plain cushions*
- *decorative fringe in matching colors*
- *color-matched thread*
- *fine needle*

SIMPLE SWAG

Embellish a country fireplace with a natural long-lasting garland.

1. Cut off a piece of thread double the length of the desired finished length of the garland. Thread it onto the needle and knot the two ends together, giving you double strength.

2. Randomly thread groups of fruit slices, leaves and cranberries onto the thread. Secure the final piece with several knots.

3. Hang across the fireplace for a decorative all-season swag. The leaves and berries will dry with time, providing a subtle color change.

INSTANT ARCHITECTURE

Classy classic accents are minutes away.

For grand traditional style on a basic budget, flank a doorway with a pair of frankly fake columns. They'll turn a modest opening into a major entrance. Glue in place. Paintable brackets can be used singly to hold *objets d'art* or paired together to form a base for a shelf. Attach to the wall with the screws that are provided with the product. Make decorative ceiling circles do other work: turn one into a richly framed mirror by taping a small piece of mirror behind the central cut-out, then mounting to the wall with Premium Glue.

SHOPPING LIST

- *polyurethane pillars, brackets and decorative ceiling mounts, available at building-supply stores*
- *Bulldog P.L. Premium Glue (do NOT use on mirror back)*
- *small piece of mirror*

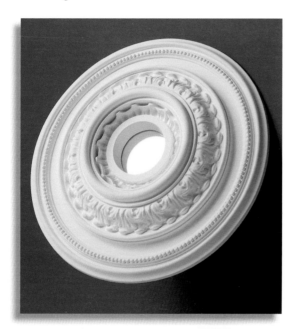

RELIEF WORK

Turn a plain column or other surface into a work of art.

1. Color the gesso, if desired, by adding colorant according to the manufacturer's instructions.

2. Spray the underside of the stencil with stencil spray and press onto the column.

3. Use a flexible spatula to press the gesso into the openings of the stencil. Carefully remove the stencil and reapply it elsewhere on the surface where it will not touch the area just decorated. Continue to apply gesso through the openings. Let the gesso dry thoroughly before touching with the stencil.

4. If desired, apply acrylic paint to the gessoed areas when it is dry. Or tint Scumble Glaze with acrylic paint or universal colorant and apply to the column.

PRINTS CHARMING

Create Old World elegance on a plain wooden tray.

SHOPPING LIST
- *wooden tray, either new or recycled*
- *fine-grit sandpaper*
- *tack cloth*
- *1-inch (2.5-cm) paintbrush*
- *latex primer paint*
- *latex semigloss paint in deep, strong color*
- *photocopy of antique print*
- *borders photocopied from a clip-art book*
- *white craft glue*
- *acrylic water-based varnish*

1. Sand the tray until very smooth, then wipe with the tack cloth to remove dust.

2. Apply one coat of primer paint. Let dry, then sand well. Remove dust with the tack cloth.

3. Apply two or three coats of semigloss paint, allowing to dry, sanding and wiping with the tack cloth between coats.

4. Have the central print and border "antique" copied at a professional photocopy shop and get it blown up (or reduced) to the exact size to fit the tray. Cut out the print and borders.

5. Apply a thin layer of glue to the underside of the central print. Press it flat in the middle of the tray, pressing out any excess glue. Wipe off excess glue with a damp cloth. Repeat with the borders. Let dry overnight.

6. Apply three coats of varnish, allowing to dry, sanding and wiping with the tack cloth between coats.

COVER UP

A sassy slipcover transforms an old stool into a star.

1. Cut out a piece of fabric that will cover the top of the stool and extend 2 inches (5 cm) down the four sides.

2. Measure the perimeter of the stool. Add 4 feet (1.2 metres) to this number. This will tell you how long a piece of fabric you must cut (or join pieces to form this length) to form the skirt and allow for pleats at the corners. To determine how deep the piece needs to be, measure from where the bottom edge of the top fabric touches the side of the stool, then add 3 inches (7.5 cm) to that number. This will allow for a 1-inch (2.5-cm) seam at the top where the bottom and top pieces join and for a double hem at the bottom.

3. Cut out and sew together the skirt fabric once you have made these calculations. Pin the skirt fabric to the top edge of the stool, tucking in 3 inches (7.5 cm) on both sides of each corner to create a deep pleat. Then, using a basting stitch, sew the corner pleats in place, but do not attach to the top piece yet.

4. Remove the skirt piece from where it is pinned to the stool and set it aside. Using basting stitches, make tiny tucks at the corners of the fabric for the top to create loose pleats as seen in the picture. Remove the top from the stool.

5. Lay the top right-side up on a flat surface. Pin the top edge of the skirt to the edge of the top, right sides together, then baste in place. Be sure the corner tucks of the top and the pleats of the skirt line up. Machine-stitch in a ½-inch (1-cm) seam.

6. Slip the cover on the stool, and mark where to sew up the hem. Remove the cover from the stool. Fold under the raw bottom edge, then press up the hem at the correct length and machine-stitch in place.

7. Insert grommets at the corners of the pleats and thread with thin cord, then tie in bows. Hand-sew decorative cord around the seam where the top and skirt meet.

HERE'S THE POINT

Create beautiful cushions from old needlepoint.

SHOPPING LIST
- *needlepoint removed from old chairs or stools*
- *tailors' chalk or marking pencil*
- *velvet fabric*
- *color-matched thread*
- *polyester stuffing*
- *cord*

---

1. Remove the needlepoint from old chairs or stools and wash it in cold-water soap. Spread it out flat on a heavy towel to dry. When still slightly damp, lay the needlepoint wrong-side up on a thick, dry towel and iron flat, stretching it into shape if it seems to be uneven.

2. Use tailors' chalk to mark where you want to cut the needlepoint to form a pleasing cushion. Machine-sew a very tight zigzag stitch along this line. (This will keep the needlework from unraveling later.) Cut out the shape about ¼ inch (0.5 cm) outside the stitching.

3. Cut a piece of velvet the same size as the needlepoint. With right sides facing, sew the two pieces together, leaving a 4-inch (10-cm) opening along one edge to insert the stuffing.

4. Turn right-side out, then fill with stuffing until comfortably fat. Hand-sew cord along the edges, tucking in the ends at the opening. Hand-sew the opening closed.

WAINSCOT A WALL

Freshen up a living room, hallway or kitchen in record time: panel it.

1. Buy the tongue-and-groove wood at hardware stores and lumberyards, packaged and precut in either 32- or 96-inch (81- or 244-cm) lengths. Packages specify how much wall space the contents will cover.

2. To prepare the walls, remove any existing baseboard and either save it to reuse or discard and replace with new. Mark a horizontal line on the wall where you want the top of the wainscotting to fall. Make sure it is level.

3. Apply caulking glue to the back of a board and press it onto the wall. Put glue on the next board and place the tongue into the groove of the first board; press it onto the wall. Repeat until the wall area is covered. Cut the boards to fit around the windows.

4. Glue or nail a cap rail to cover the top edges of the boards. Install the baseboard along the bottom edge, then paint.

TABLE MANNERS

DINING ROOMS LEND themselves to decorating with classics because they are often rooms with a single-minded focus, in which a few large-scale pieces of furniture dominate the space, and small accessories bring the rooms to life. The dining room on page 57 is a case in point. Heirloom antiques passed down through three generations gleam from years of hand polishing. Family silver and glassware, much of it two hundred years old, contributes to the sense of timelessness and continuity.

The room on page 55 is equally traditional in style, a feeling created by the elegant chandelier and matching wall sconces, the beautiful antique furniture and the classic portraits decorating the walls.

Proving that a mixture of modern and traditional classic elements creates a refreshing room, heavy silk draperies that might have been found in a 19th-century home and Regency chairs mingle with a contemporary glass-top table on page 56.

Three different country looks — all of them classics — show the warmth and appeal of these styles. The French-country

SUNNY COUNTRY DINING
Against a colorful backdrop of trellis-patterned wallpaper, a handsome antique pine flat-back cupboard and a rustic pine table establish a country theme in a casual dining room. Hoop-back chairs contribute comfort; woven baskets and brass and copper accessories provide interest.

charm evident in the dining room on page 62 comes primarily from the table, armoire and chandelier, all set within soft yellow paint and paneled walls. Canadian country exuberance expresses itself in the room on page 52 where warm pine furniture and bright yellow wallpaper and window coverings splash sunshine into the room even on a cloudy day. And finally, English-country classics, such as the framed hunting scenes and mahogany dining set, create a room reminiscent of a historic-house breakfast room on page 63. ✦

FORMAL FURNISHINGS
A crystal chandelier and matching wall sconces light a collection of fabulous 18th- and 19th-century antiques in a formal and traditional dining room. Classic portraits in oil from centuries past add to the formality. Few extraneous accessories embellish the simple gracefulness that is created by the room's exceptional antiques.

OLD AND NEW CLASSICS
The classic lines of the dining chairs and the
traditional effect of the window coverings mix
remarkably well with a handsome contemporary
glass-topped pedestal table. The gilded picture
frame, chandelier, drapery rings and hold-backs
sparkle in the midst of the super-saturated colors of
the walls, floor and fabrics. No specific period informs
the room, rather it is a collection of chic pieces which
harmonize with each other to create a timeless look.

INHERITED ELEGANCE
A Regency mirror above a dining-room fireplace
reflects family-heirloom furnishings which, wrapped
within terra-cotta walls, sparkle in the sunlight that
streams in through the big window. A collection of
cobalt-blue bottles and an antique carriage clock
decorate the mantel; a two-century-old buffet and
dining set hold other classic family treasures.

SETTLER STYLE/COUNTRY CHARM
Settler furniture from the Canadian Prairies mingles with Ontario antiques in a country dining room. Russian Mennonites crafted the two benches on arriving in Manitoba in the 1870s; whittled Ukrainian candlesticks top the two-plank Ontario pine table. The decorated chest in the foreground likely held Doukhobor settlers' effects on their journey from the Old Country. In the summer months, it would have stored bedding.

COUNTRY FURNITURE MEETS URBANE ACCESSORIES

Proving that you can mix and match in decorating, sophisticated silver accessories beautify rustic country furnishings in a small dining room. Elegant crystal decanters and silver tableware decorate the country pine harvest table, sideboard and ceiling-high corner cabinet. A brass chandelier adds sparkle; shutters cozy up the room.

FRENCH-COUNTRY FLOURISHES

French country meets city dining in an antiques-filled room. A handsome, heavily carved walnut table pairs with painted chairs, padded with berry-patterned cushions. The details of the glass-and-wood cabinet reinterpret those on the table. Overhead, a crystal chandelier dresses up in the same shades as its companion wall sconces.

ENGLISH-COUNTRY COMFORT

Mid-morning tea and late-evening dinners are equally pleasurable in a dramatic dining room, which brims with classic English country-house-style details. Boldly framed antique hunting-scene prints brighten the walls; highly polished antique furniture and a hand-crafted wrought-iron chandelier create a luxe look all day long.

DO-IT-YOURSELF

CUSHIONED COMFORT

Soften the seats of country dining chairs with quilted cushions.

SHOPPING LIST
- *old or new quilts*
- *polyester stuffing*
- *color-matched thread*
- *cord trim (optional)*
- *2 yards of 2-inch-wide (2 metres of 5-cm) ribbon for each chair (optional)*

---

1. Either cut pieces of old quilts slightly larger than the size of chair seats or make new ones to fit. (See directions on how to make a quilt on page 40). For each chair seat, you will need two pieces of quilted fabrics, 2 inches (5 cm) larger than the seat. For each cushion, lay the two pieces together right sides facing each other and pin in place. Machine-stitch around the outside edge forming a ½-inch (1-cm) hem, but leave an opening in one edge about 4 inches (10 cm) long.

2. Turn the cushion right-side out, taking care to poke into the corners so they are sharp. (You may need to trim away a little fabric in the corner hem edge to make this possible.)

3. Stuff the cushion with polyester stuffing until it is lightly puffed. Set the cushion on the chair and sit on it to determine the correct amount of filling to use.

4. Sew up the opening, then sew on decorative trim if desired.

5. To keep the cushions from falling off the chairs, you may cut 1-yard (1-metre) lengths of ribbon for each back corner. Make a fold line at the halfway point of each ribbon and sew at that fold mark attaching ribbons to two corners of the cushion.

SILVER LININGS

Whether solid sterling or plate, quality silver requires precious care.

When silver comes in contact with various compounds of sulfur, present in foods such as eggs, it tarnishes, forming a film of silver sulfide that darkens the finish. Tarnishing is also caused by oil, gas or wood heating. Regular cleaning and polishing will prevent a heavy build-up of tarnish.

Sauceboats, tureens and other such tableware should be washed with soap and warm water immediately after use. Be sure to dry silver thoroughly, since water – which contains traces of chlorine – will mark the finish.

To avoid damage to the patina and to enhance its lustre, rub silver in a gentle circular motion using a soft cloth, such as flannel. Excessive force when polishing wears the silver away. Be particularly careful around hallmarked areas. Because silver is a soft metal, easily dented or bent, large pieces should not be cleaned on a hard surface like a countertop, but should be held when polishing. Never use a brush; it will scratch and mar the finish.

Vermeil or gilt, often applied to the inside of tableware to protect the silver from staining, should be cleaned only with soap and water, never with silver polish.

If you wash silver flatware in the dishwasher, keep it separate from stainless steel. This is because a weak electric current is set up when the two metals touch, resulting in discoloration and pitting of the silver.

There are many good-quality silver polishes. Liquid and paste are convenient for all types of items, but a cleaning foam, which penetrates the grooves and crevices of more ornate pieces, can save time.

Store unused silver in tissue paper to protect it from tarnish. Camphor strips and mothballs placed with silver are also good protection as they absorb sulfur.

GIVE OLD FURNITURE A NEW LOOK
Do-it-yourself refinishing brings out wood's beauty.

SHOPPING LIST (FOR ONE TABLE)

FOR STRIPPING
- newspapers
- 4-quart (4-L) can gel stripper
- rubber gloves plus spare pair
- 1-inch (2.5-cm) paintbrush
- 4-inch (10-cm) flexible putty knife
- disposable container
- knife
- coarse steel wool
- two cloths
- laundry bleach
- 100-grit sandpaper

FOR FINISHING
- 1-quart (1-L) can transparent furniture stain
- 1-inch (2.5-cm) paintbrush
- natural-bristle brush
- satin-finish varnish or urethane
- cloth
- 1-inch (2.5-cm) sponge brush
- 400-grit sandpaper
- tack cloth

---

1. Place the piece of furniture to be stripped on a bed of newspapers three or four sheets thick. Work in a well-ventilated area away from heavy household traffic because fumes from the stripping and staining substances can make you dizzy and nauseous. Keep flammables far from furnaces and other heat sources. Wear rubber gloves because gel stripper can corrode your skin. Have a spare pair handy for when the gloves wear down.

2. Brush on two or three generous coats of stripper, enough to make the paint or the varnish drip off the sides. Leave the stripper on for the time specified by the manufacturer. Expect some melting and bubbling as well as soft crackling sounds as the old finish begins to disintegrate.

3. When the finish has softened, scrape off the coating with a flexible putty knife, in the direction of the grain. Keep a disposable container nearby to collect the goop.

4. Repeat the process with another two or three thick layers of stripper. Clean out any grooves with a knife or a cloth-wrapped scraper. Work carefully but quickly to prevent the stripper from drying.

5. Follow with a thin layer of stripper and scrape again.

6. Dip coarse steel wool in cold water and scour the surface thoroughly, in the direction of the grain, then wash with a sopping wet cloth. Scrape out the grooves again.

7. Wipe with a dry cloth. If there are darkened water stains in the wood, wipe the whole piece down with a clean cloth dipped in laundry bleach. Squeeze extra bleach onto the water marks and spread out evenly. Wipe dry, then let stand for one hour.

8. Sand the surfaces with sandpaper, in the direction of the grain, until smooth and even. Don't over-sand veneers, which are usually less than 1 mm thick.

For a traditional wood-grain finish:

1. Brush on a transparent furniture stain, in the direction of the grain. Wipe off excess with a clean, dry cloth. Let dry.

2. Use a natural-bristle brush to apply a coat of urethane. Remove drips and air bubbles with a sponge brush. Let dry and apply a second coat of varnish.

3. When dry, sand the piece along the grain with sandpaper. Wipe with the tack cloth.

4. Apply a third coat of varnish. Let dry.

Kitchens
HEART OF THE HOUSE

*D*ESIGNING A KITCHEN with classic appeal can be a challenge, although it is probably easier to succeed with one that has country elements rather than traditional details. There is a new trend towards recreating kitchens from the 1950s and 1960s, and as these more "recent" periods become chic and their furnishings and accessories become collectible, so another era of new classics emerges.

Kitchens created with country classics are joys to cook and eat in, as is proven by several shown on these pages. The comfort level is high and the welcome warm. The inspiration can be as simple as a color scheme, as with the kitchen on page 76. Here, the owner was inspired by the colors in Monet's paintings, and from this a gentle French-countryside feeling developed. This influence is seen in the backsplash and cupboard doors and carries through into the eating area beyond.

Classic French appeal also shows in the two kitchens on pages 72 and 78, where ceramic tiles, paneled doors, centre islands and cushioned chairs — all associated with classic French country — create the look.

BARN-RED BEAUTY
Wood cabinets stained barn-red, a tongue-in-groove ceiling and a maple-look laminate floor create cozy country style. An antique stained-glass window suspended from the ceiling separates the eating and food-prep areas. An apron-fronted farmhouse sink, paneled cabinets, lace curtains at the glass-paned cupboards and checkered window coverings complete the classic country look.

Classic country makes strong statements in two kitchens, too, on pages 68 and 81. In the first, reminiscent of a country barn, inviting red cupboards and checkered window treatments are featured. In the second, a colorfully painted and artfully carved pioneer cupboard and table — both made in the early 1900s on the Canadian Prairies — anchor another brilliant kitchen located in a contemporary home. In both cases, accessories finish off the classic look and add a layer of interest to the rooms. ✤

FLOWER FUN

A watermelon-green stain on paneled cabinetry and a round table lend a country air to a family kitchen. Hoop-back chairs, an ivy-wrapped chandelier and a wrought-iron-based, marble-topped serving table create additional country touches to a large, sun-filled room. A whimsical paint treatment on the floor makes flowers — inspired by the window-covering fabric — look real enough to have been tossed there.

CREATIVE COUNTRY LOOK

Paneled cabinets and painted backsplash tiles quickly create
a classic country look. When they're paired with a porcelain sink
and underpinned with dark-stained-oak flooring, the look really
comes together. The adjacent eating area provides more scope
for decorating with country flair, including patterned
wallcoverings and a carved French-Provincial dining set.

PERSIMMON PUNCH
Lacquer cabinets the color of persimmons dish up a country feast when paired with butter-yellow walls. White ceramic backsplash tiles, accented with country motifs, continue the colors found in the eating-area window coverings and chair seats (not seen). A wall of glass-fronted cabinets and raised panels decorating the doors combine for a modern interpretation of French country style.

**SUN-KISSED FROM THE
SOUTH OF FRANCE**
Sunshine-yellow backsplash tiles
and a deep greenhouse window
above the sink suggest summer
even when the thermometer
reads zero. Country-inspired
details, such as the paneled
cabinets and ceramic tiling,
provide a strong backdrop for
traditional French-country-
colored accents: blue and yellow
china, potted sunflowers and
assorted luscious fruits.

FRENCH-COUNTRY CASUAL/BIG-CITY STYLE
Inspired by the colors in a Monet painting, a large room
divides into a kitchen work area, casual eating space,
home-office niche with bookshelves and soft-seating lounge.
Myriad patterns decorate the ceramic backsplash tiles; their
colors and motifs recur, hand-painted on drawers and doors.
Terra-cotta country tiles in the kitchen area give way to the
warmth of hardwood elsewhere. The striped covering on
the sofa and yellow and blue paint on the table are direct
transports from the French countryside.

SUBTLE COUNTRY CHARM

Countless country details add up to
a kitchen brimming with charm. An
above-the-island pot hanger, whimsically
garnished with farmyard animals, holds
copper cooking utensils. Hand-painted
backsplash tiles meet tile-topped
counters. A special "antiquing" finish
on the cupboards adds to the ambience;
glass-fronted cabinet doors show off
the country motifs on the chinaware.

PAINTED PRIMITIVES

The spacious painted cupboard — constructed and carved by a Polish settler in northeastern Ontario in the 1880s — is both artful and utilitarian and perfect for holding dishes, cutlery, linens and serving pieces. In front of it, an antique Doukhobor table from Castlegar, B.C., serves many purposes. Who says new "fitted" kitchens are the best?

MINIATURE CHARM

Even a pint-sized kitchen can be infused with country charm when no detail is overlooked. And the details are many: a harvest wreath hung above fitted shutters, gleaming copper cookware on display, ceramic tiles set on the diagonal and glass-fronted cabinets revealing white chinaware. A space-saving church pew provides a place to sit for coffee and a chat; a footstool doubles as a short stepladder for reaching high-up shelves.

COUNTRY COOK-UP

Country flavor mixes with modern technology to cook up a classic kitchen. Paneled doors, a plate rack and louvred shutters create the mood; a side-by-side refrigerator, wall oven, raised dishwasher, lowered microwave and an office corner fitted with a computer, fax and television take the homey kitchen into the high-tech age but sacrifice none of the country charms.

Kitchen
PROJECTS

HAVE A HEART

Stencil a floor cloth with a heartwarming motif.

SHOPPING LIST

- *No. 10 artists' canvas (available at art supply stores)*
- *latex eggshell paint (or use acrylic craft paint) in ivory color*
- *2-inch (5-cm) foam paint roller or 2-inch (5-cm) paintbrush*
- *repositionable stencil adhesive spray*
- *long metal straight edge*
- *pencil*
- *heart-shaped stencil*
- *latex paint (or use acrylic craft paint) in pink and red*
- *½-inch (1-cm) stencil brush*
- *1-inch (2.5-cm) wide masking tape*
- *1-inch (2.5-cm) paintbrush*
- *acrylic water-based varnish*
- *scissors*
- *hot-glue gun and glue sticks*

---

1. Cut the canvas to the desired size, allowing an additional 2 inches (5 cm) on each side for shrinkage and to turn under as a hem.

2. Apply three coats of ivory-colored paint using the roller or brush, allowing it to dry between coats.

3. When dry, mark with a pencil and the metal straight edge where the heart stencil is to be first laid. Start at least 6 inches (15 cm) in from the edges to allow for the border, which will be painted last. Spray the underside of the stencil with spray adhesive. Lay it on the canvas. Using the stencil brush and red paint, dab paint inside the stencil openings creating the pattern shown in the picture. Let dry, then repeat with the pink paint. Repeat these rows until the rug is complete.

4. When the hearts are dry, use a metal straight edge and pencil to draw lines for the red border as pictured. Press masking tape along the outside edges of the border. Using the 1-inch (2.5-cm) paintbrush, apply one or two coats of red paint within the taped-off areas. Let dry, remove the masking tape, then apply three or four coats of acrylic varnish over the entire surface, allowing to dry between coats.

5. Fold over about 1 inch (2.5 cm) of the outer edges of the canvas to the underside and press with your fingers to create a crease. Cut across the corners to eliminate some bulky fabric. Use hot glue to hold the hem in place.

KITCHEN CAPER

Create your own frames for country-kitchen art.

SHOPPING LIST
- *colorful pictures for framing*
- *wood picture moldings, available at lumber stores*
- *mitre box*
- *backsaw*
- *fine-grit sandpaper*
- *tack cloth*
- *carpenters' glue*
- *four L-shaped brackets with ¼-inch-long (0.5-cm) screws to fit*
- *screwdriver*
- *small quantity of high-gloss interior latex paint*
- *1-inch (2.5-cm) paintbrush*
- *glass cut to fit frame*
- *cardboard backing*
- *eight tiny nails*
- *kraft paper*
- *screw eyes and picture wire*

1. Measure the image to be framed to calculate the amount of picture molding to buy. Using a backsaw and mitre box set at 45 degrees, cut the pieces to fit, flaring the ends of each piece to form the corners. Sand any rough edges at the corners, wipe away dust with the tack cloth and glue together.

2. When the glue is almost dry, turn the frame face-side down on a flat surface, press the joins together well and screw a bracket onto each corner. Set aside until the glue is completely dry.

3. Sand again and wipe with the tack cloth.

4. Apply at least two coats of paint. Let dry, sand and wipe between coats.

5. Place the glass, picture and backing in the frame. Nail in place on the back side. Cut a piece of kraft paper slightly smaller than the frame and glue over the back of the frame.

6. Attach screw eyes and picture wire.

(Note: If you want to have your image surrounded by a mat, take the frame and picture to a do-it-yourself framing shop and have the staff cut the mat for you. The cost will be minimal and the results will be much better than doing it at home yourself.)

RUG AND PAINT PERK-UP

Rejuvenate a country chair.

SHOPPING LIST

- *a country-look chair with removable padded wood-base seat*
- *small rag rug (one 2 x 4 foot [65 x 130 cm] rag rug will cover two chair seats)*
- *scissors*
- *needle and thread*
- *staple gun and ½-inch (1-cm) staples*
- *fine-grit sandpaper*
- *tack cloth*
- *small quantity of latex semigloss paint*
- *1-inch (2.5-cm) paintbrush*

1. Remove the chair seat and any fabric covering. Set the seat on the rug and use as a pattern to cut out the new covering, allowing about 4 inches (10 cm) extra "rug" on all sides. If the rug edges fray, sew with overcast stitching to hold them in place.

2. Lay the rug piece right-side down on a flat surface. Lay the seat, padded side against the rug. Pull the edges up and over onto the underside of the wooden seat and hold in place with staples. It is best if two people work together. Continue to staple until the rug is firmly attached to the base. Set it aside.

3. Sand the chair and wipe off the dust with the tack cloth. Apply two or three coats of paint. Let dry, sand and wipe with the tack cloth between coats.

4. Set the seat back on the chair frame and screw in place.

REST ROOMS

COLORS, FABRICS, FURNITURE and accessories combine to create classic style in the bedroom and bathroom. In many cases, reproductions of original furniture styles and fabric patterns have been adapted to contemporary tastes, but the resulting flavor is still the same as if originals had been used.

In the bedroom on this page, what could be more classic than striped wallcoverings? Combined with a tartan duvet, heirloom quilt, carved sleigh bed and framed hunting prints, the effect injects a classic, traditional English look.

Another take on a traditional classic English bedroom results from decorating a reproduction four-poster canopied bed with damask-look coverings and piling the round, skirted bedside tables with family photos and personal memorabilia (see page 91).

Town and country collide in a romantic bedroom furnished with Victorian classics, such as a black walnut bed (see page 96). Only an oil lamp lights the room.

Antiques and reproductions combine into a classic room when accessorized with updated floral chintz and over-sized

CLASSIC COMBOS
Several classic elements — striped wallcoverings topped by a border depicting foxes and hounds, hunting-scene prints, a pair of antique sleigh beds, tartan duvet covers and an heirloom quilt hanging on a vintage blanket stand — combine into a classy chic bedroom. A well-worn carpet anchors the elements.

checked fabric. The disparate items — many of them classics — are eclectic, but it is this very factor that energizes the room and prevents a static feeling (see pages 92 and 93).

It's the handwoven coverlet on the four-poster bed and a collection of blue accessories that imbue the room on pages 94 and 95 with a colonial American feeling. Everything in the room is a reproduction of earlier classic furniture; but some of it is scaled down to fit the smaller-sized bedrooms prevalent in today's homes. ⊗

CANOPIED CLASSIC
Who doesn't dream of a classic English bedroom reminiscent of the Middle Ages whose centrepiece is a canopied, carved four-poster bed? This romantic room contains many embellishments, none of them antiques, to complete the "antique" look: generous fabric-skirted side tables topped with family photos and reading lamps fitted with custom shades, a cozy comforter and stacks of pillows.

ROMANCE IN THE RED

Classic antiques and accessories, paired with traditional floral and over-sized checked fabrics, promise a traditional bedroom with enormous charm. The scroll top of a trellis headboard repeats the sensuous curves of the antique bedside bouliotte lamp. The ginger-jar lamp on the other side repeats the images in the framed prints hanging above the bed. An 18th-century rocking chair and a Victorian footstool in the foreground spell out romance.

COLONIAL CLASSIC

A handwoven spread covers a four-poster bed, while a color-matched quilt stands by for extra warmth in a charming pastel-blue bedroom. A collection of plates decorates the wall, backed by a traditional blue bow-and-ribbon accent. Botanical prints, a carriage clock and a dried-flower arrangement harmoniously complete the classic colonial look.

VICTORIAN ROMANCE

A black walnut bed, crisply carved in a classic late-Victorian manner, gets star treatment when set on the diagonal in a high-ceilinged bedroom. A plaid woven throw and cushion covers made from the same material add color to the white quilted bedcovering. Antique accessories create a historically inspired mood.

POINTED PUNCH

Bold awning stripes never pass out of style or fade in popularity, making them one of the most enduring classic motifs. Here, they add punch to an otherwise neutral bathroom. A traditionally patterned hand-knotted rug incorporating the colors of the shower curtain and the tiles both warms up and softens the chilly sleekness of the flooring.

BLUE AND WHITE BATHING BEAUTY
A wealth of classic touches, both large and small, create a country-style bathroom that also overflows with city chic. Tiny blue flowers on the tiles and sinks reappear in the accessories that decorate the tier of glass shelves, the paneled-door knobs, the towel-holding basket and the sink-side chinaware. Midnight-blue ceramic tiles cover the floor.

Bedrooms & Bathrooms

PROJECTS

STAR STRUCK

Three stellar sew-it projects.

SHOPPING LIST
- *1-½ yards of 1-yard-wide (1.4 metres of 1-metre) quilted fabric for each project*
- *color-matched thread*
- *5 yards (4.5 metres) bias binding*
- *decorative star trims*

HIDE A NIGHTIE IN A LACY PAJAMA BAG

1. Decide how large the bag will be and cut fabric to size. Lay the fabric wrong-side up on a flat surface with a short end facing you. Take this short end and fold it two-thirds the way up the piece. Pin the sides together. Cut a curve along the top edge to form a neat flap as shown in the picture.

2. Machine-sew bias binding to attach the sides together and to finish off the edge of the flap's curved end. Hand-sew gathered lace to the underside of the curved edge. Sew on stars and a tassel. Store pajamas in it and decorate your bed.

SEW A GLAMOROUS PILLOW

1. Measure the pillow to be covered. Cut two pieces of quilted fabric 1 inch (2.5 cm) larger than the pillow. Machine- or hand-sew stars where desired on the fabric. Lay the two pieces of fabric, right sides together, on a flat surface. Pin the edges together. Machine-sew a ½-inch (1-cm) seam all around, leaving an opening through which to stuff the pillow. Turn the cover right-side out.

2. Stuff the pillow into the cover and hand-sew the opening closed. Hand-sew on decorative trim.

CURL UP WITH A VIDEO BLANKET

1. Machine-sew bias binding around the edges of the quilted fabric.

2. Hand- or machine-sew decorative stars where desired.

MIDAS TOUCH

Create dazzle with gold leaf.

1. Sand the object(s) to be gilded with sandpaper and wipe clean with the tack cloth.

2. Apply one coat of dark paint. Let dry, then sand lightly and wipe clean with the tack cloth.

3. Apply a thin layer of size. Let dry for about an hour or until the surface feels tacky.

4. Very carefully remove one piece of gold leaf from the package and lay it on the tacky surface. Press it lightly into any contours, using a soft brush. Set aside for two to three hours.

5. Use the soft brush or cloth to flick off loose bits of gold leaf. Some of the color underneath will likely be exposed, creating an antiqued effect.

6. Apply varnish to surfaces that will get a lot of wear, such as trays.

COUNTRY QUILT ART

Hang quilt squares for instant art.

SHOPPING LIST

- *old quilts*
- *canvas stretcher frames (available at art supply stores), sized to fit the quilt blocks*
- *staple gun and ¼-inch (0.5-cm) staples*

---

1. Wash old quilts and let dry, then cut into blocks. (Or make new blocks, following directions for making a quilt on page 40.) To keep the edges from fraying, either hand-stitch or machine-sew an overcast stitch along them.

2. Assemble the stretcher frames. Extend the outer edges of the quilt block around to the back of the frame and staple in place, pulling the fabric taut. Hang on the wall.

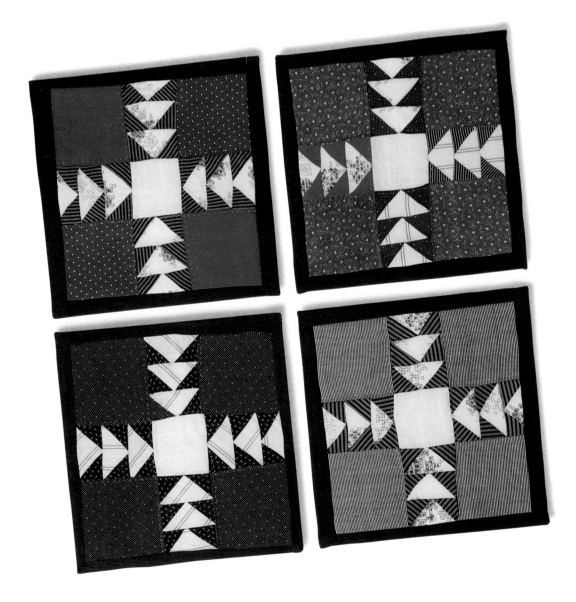

BERRY NICE BREAKFAST TRAY

Pretty up a plain tray with stencils.

SHOPPING LIST

- *plain wooden tray*
- *fine-grit sandpaper*
- *tack cloth*
- *1-inch (2.5-cm) paintbrush*
- *cream-colored latex semigloss paint*
- *ruler and pencil*
- *¾-inch (2-cm) masking tape*
- *strawberry stencil*
- *repositionable stencil adhesive spray*
- *two (2-oz/59-mL) bottles acrylic craft paint, one red and one green*
- *small stencil brush*
- *acrylic varnish*

1. Sand the tray and wipe clean with the tack cloth. Paint with three coats of semigloss paint. Let dry, sand and wipe clean between coats.

2. Use the ruler and pencil to draw the two green borders onto the surface of the tray. Press masking tape along the outer edges of these markings. Fill in the spaces between with green paint. Let dry, then remove the tape.

3. Spray the underside of the stencil with adhesive and press it onto the tray.

4. Apply paints through the stencil as shown in the picture. Let dry.

5. Apply three coats of varnish. Let dry, sand lightly and wipe clean between coats.

OLD-FASHIONED HEADBOARD

Put a quilt to work as a headboard.

SHOPPING LIST

- *a quilt*
- *satin ribbon approx. 3 or 4 inches (7 or 10 cm) wide ***
- *1½-inch-diameter (3.8-cm) wooden drapery rod (length of pole depends on widths of bed and quilt), finials and wall-mount brackets*
- *fine-grit sandpaper*
- *tack cloth*
- *1-inch (2.5-cm) paintbrush*
- *one (2-oz/59-mL) bottle acrylic craft paint in color taken from quilt*
- *one (2-oz/59-mL) bottle acrylic varnish*
- ** The ribbon needs to be wide enough that when it is sewn onto the back of the quilt, the drapery rod can pass through the "tunnel." It needs to be long enough to stretch across the edge of the quilt.*

---

1. Lay out the quilt to be sure it stretches the width of the bed. Machine-sew the ribbon to the back of the quilt along the "top" edge. Sew as close to both edges of the ribbon as possible in order to create a "tunnel."

2. Sand the rod, finials and brackets. Wipe clean with the tack cloth. Paint with two or three coats of paint. Let dry. Sand and wipe clean between coats. Apply one coat of varnish. Let dry.

3. Mount the brackets on the wall at the desired height and width at the head of the bed. Thread the rod through the tunnel on the back of the quilt. Hang on the brackets.

MARVELOUS MAKEOVER

Transform a tattered castoff into an elegant boudoir table.

SHOPPING LIST

- *an old table; kidney-shaped is best*
- *fine-grit sandpaper*
- *tack cloth*
- *one can glossy spray paint, gray*
- *pencil*
- *small can of size*
- *one packet each of faux gold leaf and faux silver leaf*
- *one (2-oz/59-mL) bottle silver acrylic craft paint*
- *one can Penetrol glaze*
- *turpentine*
- *¼-inch (0.5-cm) paintbrush*
- *1-inch (2.5-cm) paintbrush*
- *silver-colored rickrack trim*
- *water-based tacky craft glue*
- *images cut from magazines or cards*
- *one small can urethane, gloss finish*
- *fine steel wool*
- *polyester voile fabric*
- *netting fabric*
- *½-inch (2-cm) wide Velcro™*
- *ribbon, fabric flowers, buttons, etc.*

1. Sand the table until smooth. Wipe with the tack cloth to remove any dust.

2. Evenly spray the table with gray paint.

3. Draw a diamond pattern on top with the pencil. Apply size with the ¼-inch (0.5-cm) brush along the lines or wherever you want gold leaf to adhere. Set aside for 30 to 45 minutes or until the size feels tacky. Tear gold leaf into small strips, the width of the size-painted areas, and press onto the surface. Brush off any extra leaf. Let dry.

4. Apply size to areas between the gold leaf or wherever you want silver leaf to be. Set aside until the size feels tacky, then apply silver leaf in the same way as the gold. Let dry.

5. Dab silver paint randomly over the surface. Let dry.

6. Sprinkle a little Penetrol glaze and turpentine over top. Spread around using a 1-inch (2.5-cm) paint-brush. Then, using the ¼-inch (0.5-cm) brush, gently dab it all over the surface to create a distressed effect. Let dry.

7. Glue rickrack trim around the edges. Glue on small images where desired. Let dry, then apply at least three coats of urethane, allowing to dry between coats. After the final coat, rub lightly with fine steel wool.

8. Make a skirt. Measure the perimeter of the table and multiply that figure by three. You will need to sew panels of fabric together to produce a single piece that wide. Its depth should be the height of the table plus 12 inches (30 cm) for a deep hem. Buy sufficient net and voile fabric.

9. Machine-sew net and voile together along the top edge. Fold over ¾ inch (2 cm) and machine-sew the folded edge in place with long running stitches. Pull up the thread to create gathers to make the skirt fit around the table. Topstitch through all layers. Sew one part of Velcro™ to the underside of the gathers. Glue the other part to the tabletop edge. Attach the skirt to the table.

10. Turn up the hem of the net and voile separately and hand-sew in place.

Dens
A STUDIED LOOK

$\mathcal{D}$ECORATING A DEN or library is easy when classic furnishings, accessories and colors are brought into play. Consider the purpose of the room: it is generally used to work in or to settle back and relax, read or study.

The classic library opposite provides for all these activities. Three armchairs of classic design and proportion make sure there are places to read comfortably. An antique drop-leaf Duncan Phyfe-style table opens up for spreading out work. Wall-to-wall shelves in a traditional style hold books; the wallcovering above is a timeless traditional from the turn of the century.

Looking more like the interior of a private and exclusive men's club than a den in a small private home, the room on page 113 is so successful because of its myriad classic elements. Paneled walls have existed for centuries, helping to cosset visitors to a room. Tartan and striped fabrics likewise are classics. Wingback chairs bring to mind centuries past when their enfolding shape kept the sitter warm in unheated rooms. Though none of these elements is "old" or an antique, still, the resulting combination creates a classic room.

Totally different, but still a classic, is the sunny country den created under attic eaves and shown on page 112. True country antiques, updated with contemporary country furniture, combine to create the look. A brightly slipcovered sofa and cushy carpet provide comfort when reflective work takes precedence over desk tasks. ❂

ENGLISH COUNTRY-HOUSE STYLE
Comfortable chairs and a wealth of antiques combine in a spacious library, which looks as though it could be the favorite room in an English country home. A drop-leaf pedestal Duncan Phyfe-style table does double duty holding lamps and accessories behind the sofa; it can be opened out for working on or to spread out books and maps. Wall-to-wall bookshelves painted in the same pristine color as the moldings and trim provide relief from the dark walls.

ATTIC OFFICE

A fully functioning office tucked under the eaves brims with classic country charm and laid-back character. Strong sun-drenched colors each hold their own when paired with equally strong motifs, such as on the chair cushion and patterned rug. A whimsical lamp interprets a traditional shape in heavy metal; a wicker filing cabinet replaces the more ubiquitous metal variety.

MEN'S CLUB LIBRARY

Don't-be-shy shades in a club-like den create a room that's spunky, cozy, classic and welcoming. Blazer-blue stripes on the wing chair meet mixed-to-match tartan on the three-seater sofa. Sink-in cushions convene on the window seat. Paneled walls and small-paned windows add to the feeling of being in a private Victorian men's club.

Dens
PROJECTS

LUXE LAMPSHADE
Create an elegant shade for an elegant lamp.

> ### SHOPPING LIST
> - *1 yard (1 metre) medium- to heavy-weight fabric*
> - *plain lampshade*
> - *six or eight large paper clips*
> - *contact cement*
> - *1-inch (2.5-cm) brush*
> - *ribbon*
> - *decorative baubles*
> - *thread*

1. Lay the fabric over the shade and roughly cut the shape out of the fabric. Fine-tune the shape by temporarily attaching the fabric to the shade with large paper clips, then cutting so that the fabric fits the shape of the shade with an additional 1 inch (2.5 cm) all around for turning under.

2. Lay the fabric wrong-side up on a flat surface. Spread with a thin coat of contact cement according to the manufacturer's instructions. Brush a thin layer of contact cement on the shade. Let dry until tacky.

3. Press the fabric in place, turning the raw edges under so that the shade is neat.

4. Use contact cement as directed to attach ribbon, then sew on baubles.

BRUSH-UPS
Paint fireplace tiles to update their look.

SHOPPING LIST
- *ceramic tile fireplace surround*
- *trisodium phosphate (TSP)*
- *small artists' brush*
- *DecoArt UltraGloss Air Dry Enamel Paint*

1. Wash the tiles with a solution of TSP, according to the manufacturer's instructions, to remove grime and smoke deposits. Wash with clear water and wipe dry.

2. Use a small artists' brush to apply the paint. Let dry for several days before touching it.

GET A FOOT UP

Use a crate to create a relaxing footstool.

SHOPPING LIST

- *small wooden crate, about 12 inches (30 cm) square*
- *four 3-inch (7.5-cm) wooden balls with one flat side and screws (available at craft stores)*
- *supplies for crackle finish (see mirror page 18)*
- *furniture wax and soft cloth*
- *four tassels (optional)*
- *decorative cord (optional)*
- *hot-glue gun and glue sticks*
- *ready-made cushion sized to fit*

1. Beautify the basic box: either give it a crackle-finish treatment following the instructions on page 18 or rub it with several coats of furniture polish, applied with a soft cloth. Treat the four feet the same way, then screw the feet to the four corners of the box.

2. Attach tassels and cord to the top edge of the box with hot glue.

3. Stuff the cushion into the box and puff it out the top.

DO-IT-YOURSELF

SHOPPING LIST
- *a wooden picture frame, preferably one with some ridges in it*
- *fine-grit sandpaper*
- *piece of medium-weight fabric, such as silk or brocade, and/or kraft paper bigger than the frame*
- *fabric marker or pencil*
- *scissors*
- *white craft glue*
- *kraft knife*
- *decorative cord for trim (optional)*
- *hot-glue gun and glue sticks*
- *kraft paper for backing*
- *small screw eyes and picture wire*

ELEGANT WRAP

Recycle a frame with a remnant of fabric or kraft paper.

FABRIC FRAME

1. Sand any rough edges off the frame.

2. To cover the frame with fabric, lay the fabric wrong-side up on a flat surface, top with the frame. Trace around the frame with a fabric marker or pencil. Cut out a piece of fabric about 2 inches (5 cm) bigger than the frame on all sides. Cut out some of the fabric from the inside portion, but leave enough to wrap around to the back side of the frame. Cut into the fabric where it will fall at the inner corners of the frame.

3. Spread craft glue in a thin, even layer all over the front and inner and outer edges of the frame. Lay the fabric on top, right-side up. Press it firmly onto the frame, taking care to smooth it out and tuck it in neatly in and around the inner and outer edges. Let dry.

4. Trim the fabric so that when you wrap it around to the back side of the frame, it will appear tidy and uniform in size. Cut across the outer corners of the fabric to reduce the amount of fabric being glued down. Be sure the cuts in the fabric into the inner corners permit the fabric to lie flat and taut.

5. Apply a thin layer of craft glue to the back side of the frame. Press the fabric in place. Let dry.

6. Using a hot-glue gun, attach decorative cord around the outer edge of the frame. Set aside to dry.

7. Cut out a piece of kraft paper slightly smaller than the frame. Use craft glue to attach the paper on the underside to cover the fabric edges. Attach screw eyes and picture wire for hanging.

KRAFT PAPER FRAME

1. Sand any rough edges off the frame. Taking a piece of kraft paper about one and a half times the size of the frame, crush it by repeatedly scrunching it into a ball for about five or ten minutes, or until it is very soft and pliable. Do not stretch it or it might tear; repeated scrunching will soften it until it has a fabric-like feel.

2. Lay the paper on a flat surface and smooth it out so it lies flat but shows plenty of texture from its wrinkles. Follow the directions above, steps 2 through 7

THE GREAT DIVIDE

A romantic hanging panel adds elegance and style to any doorway.

SHOPPING LIST

- *four pieces select pine wood, 1x2x84 inches*
- *four pieces select pine wood, 1x2x24 inches*
- *two pieces select pine wood, 1x2x21 inches*
- *eight decorative wood corner brackets*
- *one wood curtain pole, 1⅜ x 48 inches (3.4 x 90 cm)*
- *one wood finial*
- *two wood curtain rings*
- *two wood mounting brackets*
- *1½-inch (3.8-cm) finishing nails*
- *1¾-inch (4-cm) flathead screws*
- *corrugated metal fasteners*
- *wood glue and wood filler*
- *sandpaper*
- *two white threaded hooks*
- *2 yards (2 metres) sheer fabric, 118-inch-wide (300-cm)*
- *1 quart (1 L) oil-base primer paint*
- *1 quart (1 L) low-lustre enamel paint*
- *white caulking*
- *mitre box*

1. Build two frames and mount the fabric between them. Using a mitre box, saw the corners of the 24-inch (60-cm) long and 84-inch (210-cm) long pine pieces at 45 degree angles. Glue the corners together. Hold with a framing vice and hammer a corrugated fastener across each joint and a 1½-inch (3.8-cm) finishing nail into the outside edges of the frame. Glue the 21-inch (52-cm) long crossbar in the centre of the frame, then hammer in place with a corrugated fastener and the finishing nails at the outer edge. Countersink the nails.

2. Set the corner brackets in place. Use small nails to hold temporarily. Drill holes through the frame into the brackets, then screw together using the flathead screws. Fill the holes with wood filler, then sand. Paint with primer and, when dry, sand again. Apply two coats of low-lustre enamel paint.

3. Lay the fabric on top of one of the frames. Mark the top and bottom edges and centre the crossbar. Machine-sew a double row of long stitches across the fabric width so they will be hidden by the top and bottom bars of the frame and the crossbar. Pull up the threads so the gathered fabric fits within the frame. Leave several inches at the top and bottom beyond the stitching to make mounting to the frame easier. Use a staple gun to attach the gathered fabric to the top and bottom of one of the frames and to the crossbar, pulling it taut. Trim the excess.

4. Lay the second frame on top of the fabric, wrong sides together. Nail to the first frame using 1½-inch (3.8-cm) finishing nails.

5. Attach the two threaded hooks to the top of the screen about 4 inches (10 cm) in from each end. Cut the wood pole to the desired length. Attach the finial. Thread with the wood rings. Screw the wood-mounting brackets to the pole, then screw the brackets to the ceiling. Hook the screen onto the wood rings and adjust the threaded hooks to make the screen hang evenly.

INDEX

CREDITS

DESIGNERS

William Anderson
416/536-8011
page 17

Katherine S. Brown
416/233-8727
pages 10, 60-61, 66, 80, 94-95

Canac Kitchens
905/881-2153
pages 82-83

Suzanne Davison Interior Design Inc.
416/481-5254
pages 15, 112

Dinnick Designs
416/323-9754
page 46

Reg Dohms, Luxe
416/463-0215
pages 47, 100-101

Jill Drinkwater
Ambridge Ferazzutti
416/975-8664
pages 48-49

Douglas Gill Ltd.
519/672-6001
pages 25, 71

Gloria Hugo Designs
416/925-3578
page 24

Karen Large Design
613/798-0115
pages 28, 110

Carolyn Mahovlich, Design.
519/472-9937
pages 106-107

Diane Manor-Owens, Elaine Schmitt
and Gayle Weatherhead
613/822-0557
page 29

John McAuley & Associates Inc.
416/652-5556
page 13

Moya McPhail Design
905/885-1567
pages 50-51, 56, 108-109

Sharon Mimran
416/785-1003
pages 72-73

Barbara Munn
Yorkville Design Centre
416/922-6620
pages 74-75

Susan Polak Interior Design
416/489-6105
pages 22-23, 26-27, 30-31, 34-35,
92-23, 120-121

Patti Prest
416/233-8327
page 105

Jan Regis, CBD CKD
Binns Designers Kitchens & Bath
1-877-509-5555
page 68

Ritins Studio
416/467-8920
page 45

Splash Bathrooms
416/242-2442
pages 77, 97

Zuzana Wilemova Design
416/461-4016
pages 114-115, 118-119

Patricia Witiw Designs
416/769-1969
page 76

Photographers

Linda Corbett: pages 16, 86, 118

Evan Dion: pages 15, 18, 42, 44, 45, 50-51, 56, 65, 102-103, 104, 109, 117, 120-121

Colin Erricson: page 115

Karen Levy: pages 48-49, 107

Michael Mahovlich: pages 46, 47, 100-101, 105

John O'Brien: page 87

Christopher Reardon: page 57

Ted Yarwood: front cover, pages 10, 13, 14, 17, 19, 20, 22-23, 24, 25, 26-27, 28, 29, 30-31, 32-33, 34-35, 36, 37, 38-39, 41, 43, 52, 55, 58-59, 60-61, 62, 63, 66, 68, 71, 72-73, 74-75, 76, 77, 78-79, 80, 81, 82-83, 85, 88, 91, 92-93, 94-95, 96, 97, 98-99, 110, 112, 113, 116

Look for these titles in the CHATELAINE food express series

NEW TWISTS for
100 everyday foods
from apples to zucchini.
Includes a survival guide and
a comprehensive index.

INCLUDES a special section on
off-beat grilling, such as pizza,
cornish hens and jambalaya.
Plus indoor adaptations for
year-round sizzle.

INCLUDES favorite recipes
frequently requested by
CHATELAINE readers. Plus a
large section devoted entirely
to chocolate.

THE A TO Z LISTING of ingredients
returns in *Quickies 2*. This time
the focus is on vegetables, beans
and grains. Includes a seasonal
survival guide.

FROM APPETIZERS to salads
to soups, impress from the
very first bite. Includes dips,
spreads & salsas, risottos
and festive recipes.

CHATELAINE
home decor
CLASSIC CHIC

FOR SMITH SHERMAN BOOKS INC.

EDITORIAL DIRECTOR
Carol Sherman

ART DIRECTOR
Andrew Smith

SENIOR EDITOR
Bernice Eisenstein

PAGE LAYOUT AND COMPOSITION
Joseph Gisini

DESIGN ASSISTANCE
Jonathan Freeman

COLOR SEPARATIONS
T-C4 Graphics Ltd., Winnipeg

PRINTING
Kromar Printing Ltd., Winnipeg

SMITH SHERMAN BOOKS INC.
533 College Street, Suite 402,
Toronto, Canada M6G 1A8
e-mail: bloke@total.net

FOR CHATELAINE

CHATELAINE ADVISORY BOARD
Rona Maynard
Lee Simpson

PROJECT MANAGER
Cheryl Smith

CHATELAINE, MACLEAN HUNTER
PUBLISHING LIMITED
777 Bay Street,
Toronto, Canada M5W 1A7
e-mail: letters@chatelaine.com